DIGI-KNOW?!:

THE OFFICIAL BOOK OF

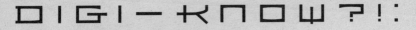

DIGITAL DIGIMON MONSTERS

FACTS AND FUN

BY MICHAEL TEITELBAUM

SCHOLASTIC IN...

New York Toronto London Au...
Mexico City New Delhi H...

D0381433

ISBN 0-439-22225-7

12 11 10 9 8 7 6 5 4 3 2 1   0 1 2 3 4/0

Printed in the U.S.A.
First Scholastic printing, December 2000

TABLE OF CONTENTS

INTRODUCTION

ENTER . . .

AN INCREDIBLE WORLD

Boot up and step into the astonishing world of Digimon. But proceed with caution.

Can you survive on File Island?

Will your Digimons digivolve?

Can you tell a good Digimon from a bad one?

Your success in navigating the virtual twists and turns of DigiWorld — not to mention this book — will depend on your knowledge of the Digital Monsters, good and evil, that inhabit this digital world.

What level you achieve — In-Training, Rookie, Champion, or Ultimate — will depend on how well you know the ins and outs of all things Digi!

Get ready to download gigabytes of fun!

BACKSPACE ...
TO WHERE IT ALL
BEGAN

It started innocently enough.

Seven kids were having a ball at summer camp. Then suddenly it began to snow — in the middle of July! This was their first clue that something very weird was going on. None of them, however, had any idea just *how* weird things were about to get.

Brilliant streaks of rainbow-colored light poured down from the sky surrounding the seven campers. With a blinding flash, they were suddenly transported from the comfortable, friendly, familiar world they all knew into a bizarre new reality — the Digital World. This eerie place — called DigiWorld — seemed oddly familiar, yet very different from any place they had ever been.

And then things got even weirder! Each of the

seven kids — **Tai**, the leader; **Sora**, the brave but cautious one; **Matt**, Mr. Cool; **T.K.**, Matt's sweet little brother; **Izzy**, the computer whiz; **Mimi**, daddy's little princess; and **Joe**, the worrywart — met small friendly creatures who instantly became their pals.

These strange but friendly life-forms were the Digimons — Digital Monsters — that inhabit Digi-World. But the kids quickly discovered that not all Digimons are cute and friendly. Some are evil and really, really nasty. Still others are usually nice, but are being controlled by evil Digimons.

And so the adventure in DigiWorld began.

SHIFT ...
INTO DIGI—MODE

But if you're a Digimon fan, you probably know all this! Plus a whole lot more about these incredible creatures, the seven Digidestined kids who enter their world, and the fantastic DigiWorld itself. But how much do you *really* know?

This book is filled with cool questions, quizzes, puzzles, jokes, and tons of fun and facts about all things Digi. Of course, the answers are provided at the end of the book, but it's more fun if you don't peek! See if you can meet the challenge.

CONTROL . . . YOUR DIGI-IQ

Are **you** Digidestined? Are you the world's biggest Digimon fan? How much do you really know about Tai, Sora, Matt, T.K., Izzy, Mimi, and Joe? And how much do you know about all the Digimons, the stages through which they digivolve, the evil Digimons, and the entire DigiWorld? Check out the fill-ins, true-and-false quizzes, multiple choice questions, and puzzles to find out. It's time to grab your Digivice and dive into DigiWorld!

When you're finished, give yourself one point for each correct answer. Then, using the key on the last page of the book, find out if you are In-Training, a Rookie, a Champion, or an Ultimate.

Good luck!

DOT-TO-DOT, DIGI-TO-DIGI I

Connect the dots on this page to meet the leader of the Digidestined children. Then connect the dots on each of the next three pages to see this kid's Digimon digivolve.

Connect the dots on this page to meet a Micro Type, In-Training-level Digimon, who is partner to the kid on the previous page.

· 7

20 ·

6 ·
· 8

19 ·

5 ·
· 9
· 21

4 ·
18 ·
10 ·
17 · · 22
· 3 · 11
· 16 · 23
2 ·
14 · · 15 · 24
· 1 · 12

36 ·
· 13 · 25
26

35 ·
· 27

34 ·
· 28

33 ·
· 29

32 ·
30 ·
31 ·

Connect the dots on this page to meet a Reptile Type, Rookie-level Digimon, who digivolves from the Digimon on the previous page.

Connect the dots on this page to meet a Dinosaur Type, Champion-level Digimon, who digivolves from the Digimon on the previous page.

DIGI-QUIZ 1

When the seven Digidestined kids arrive in Digi-World they discover all types of Digimons. How much do *you* know about all these amazing monsters? Find out in this first Digi-Quiz.

Circle the correct answer: A, B, or C.

 The Digimon that Tai first finds in DigiWorld is:

A. Koromon

B. Tsunomon

C. Motimon

 The Digimon that Matt first finds in DigiWorld is:

A. Tentomon

B. Patamon

C. Tsunomon

3 The Digimon that Sora first finds in DigiWorld is:

A. Angemon

B. Yokomon

C. Birdamon

4 The Digimon that Izzy first finds in DigiWorld is:

A. Zudomon

B. Motimon

C. Lillymon

 5 The Digimon that T.K. first finds in DigiWorld is:

A. Tokomon

B. Bukamon

C. Agumon

6 The Digimon that Mimi first finds in DigiWorld is:

A. Palmon

B. Greymon

C. Tanemon

7 The Digimon that Joe first finds in DigiWorld is:

A. Bukamon

B. Gomamon

C. Togemon

The evil Digimon that looks like a giant red beetle is:

A. Seadramon

B. Kuwagamon

C. Meramon

 The Digimon that looks like a giant metal dinosaur is:

A. Monzaemon

B. Numemon

C. Monochromon

10 The Digimon that looks like a man of flames is:

A. Devimon

B. Sukamon

C. Meramon

11 The android Digimon that looks like a giant robot is:

A. Andromon

B. Bakemon

C. Leomon

12 The Digimon that looks like a giant Teddy Bear is:

A. Ogremon

B. Monzaemon

C. Elecmon

13 The Digimon that looks like a unicorn is:

A. Unimon

B. Whamon

C. Gazimon

14 The Digimon that looks like a lion is:

A. Etemon

B. Leomon

C. Drimogemon

15 The Digimon that has the hooves of a horse and wears an iron mask is:

    A. Centarumon

    B. Pagumon

    C. Cockatrimon

 16 The evil Digimon that looks like a ghost with big teeth is:

    A. Piximon

    B. Datamon

    C. Bakemon

 17 The evil Digimon that looks like a giant rabbit is:

    A. Devimon

    B. Gazimon

    C. Vegiemon

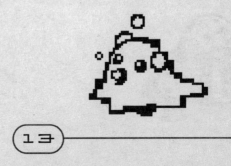

18 The Digimon that looks like a whale is:

A. Whamon

B. Gekomon

C. Myotismon

19 The evil Digimon that looks like a chicken is:

A. Dokugumon

B. Kokatorimon

C. Gatomon

20 The evil Digimon that looks like a giant walking brain is:

A. Gesomon

B. Mammothmon

C. Vademon

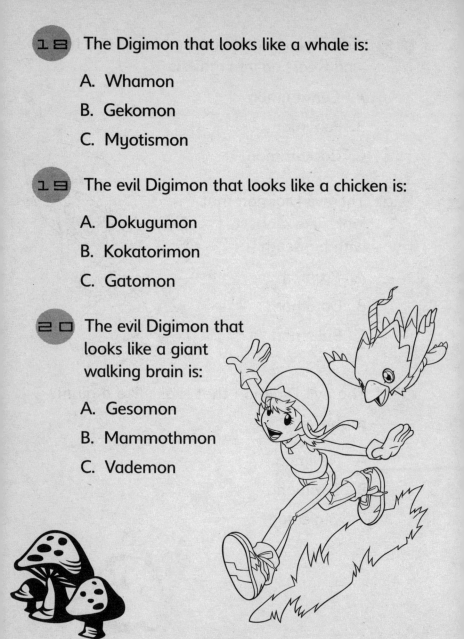

DIGI-MATCH

Match each of the seven children on the left-hand side of the page with his or her Digimon on the right-hand side of the page.

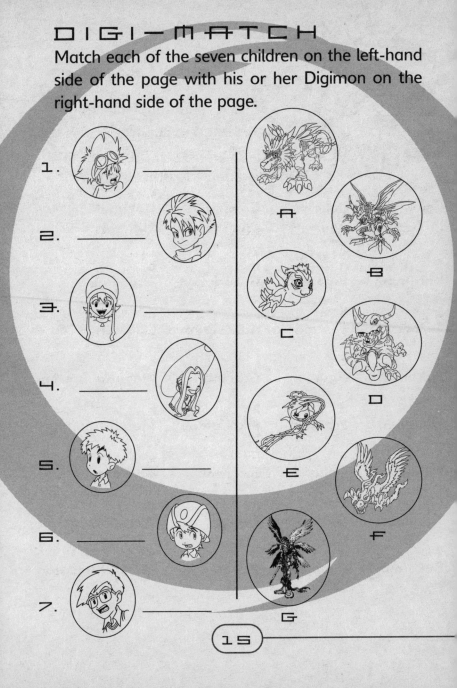

1. _____

2. _____

3. _____

4. _____

5. _____

6. _____

7. _____

A

B

C

D

E

F

G

15

DIGIVOLUTION MATCH-UP

Match each In-Training-level Digimon listed in column 1 with its Rookie, Champion, and Ultimate forms listed in the other columns.

Column 1: In-Training	Column 2: Rookie	Column 3: Champion	Column 4: Ultimate
1 _____ _____ _____ Koromon	**a** Biyomon	**h** Garurumon	**o** Zudomon
2 _____ _____ _____ Tsunomon	**b** Tentomon	**i** Kabuterimon	**p** Lillymon
3 _____ _____ _____ Yokomon	**c** Agumon	**j** Greymon	**q** MegaKabuterimon
4 _____ _____ _____ Tanemon	**d** Patamon	**k** Ikkakumon	**r** MetalGreymon
5 _____ _____ _____ Motimon	**e** Gabumon	**l** Birdramon	**s** Garudamon
6 _____ _____ _____ Tokomon	**f** Gomamon	**m** Togemon	**t** WereGarurumon
7 _____ _____ _____ Bukamon	**g** Palmon	**n** Angemon	**u** MagnaAngemon

DIGI-CLOSE-UP

Zoom in for a really, really close view of your favorite Digimon. Can you figure out which Digimon is which?

SCRAMBLED NAMES

Devimon has used his evil power to scramble the names of ten Digimon. Help Tai and his friends by unscrambling the ten names.

1) OZDUONM_____
(hint: Joe's Ultimate Digimon)

2) NLILOMLY_____
(hint: Mimi's Ultimate Digimon)

3) SONUTOMN_____
(hint: Matt's In-Training Digimon)

4) KANKIMKUO_____
(hint: Joe's Champion Digimon)

5) GANOMU_____
(hint: Tai's Rookie Digimon)

6) RANUROMUG_____
(hint: Matt's Champion Digimon)

7) NOTENOTM_____
(hint: Izzy's Rookie Digimon)

8) MITUBAKENOR_____
(hint: Izzy's Champion Digimon)

9) KABNOUM_____
(hint: Joe's In-Training Digimon)

10) TOMINOM_____
(hint: Izzy's In-Training Digimon)

DIGI-GRID PICTURE SEARCH

Help Yokomon digivolve to Birdramon! In the grid below, circle the three stages of her digivolution (Yokomon, Biyomon, Birdramon) when they appear in the exact order shown here. Search up, down, left, right, and diagonally.

The exact order:

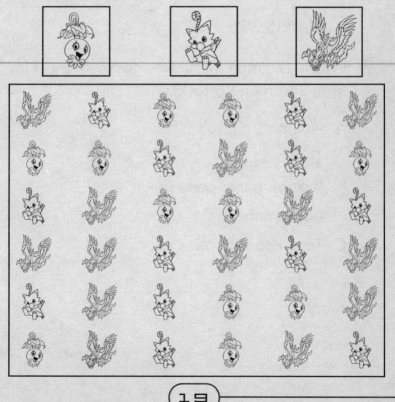

DIGI-QUIZ II

Here you go, your second Digi-Quiz. Circle the correct answer: A, B, or C.

1 Who is the first evil Digimon the kids encounter when they arrive in DigiWorld?

A. Seadramon

B. Meramon

C. Kuwagamon

2 Which Digimon digivolves to save the kids from Shellmon's attack?

A. Agumon digivolves to Greymon.

B. Bukamon digivolves to Gomamon.

C. Tanemon digivolves to Palmon.

3 Which giant metal Dinosaur Type Digimon is battling with his lookalike for control of his territory?

A. Birdramon

B. Monochromon

C. Meramon

4 When the Digidestined crew camp out in a deserted bus by a lake, which giant Digimon is the bus parked on top of?

A. Seadramon

B. Devimon

C. Ogremon

5 When Tai and his friends fall into the lake, who defeats the giant Digimon by digivolving?

A. Palmon digivolves to Togemon.

B. Gabumon digivolves to Garurumon.

C. Tentomon digivolves to Kabuterimon.

6 In the village of Yokomon, the kids find a volcano guarded by which flaming Digimon?

A. Meramon

B. Kuwagamon

C. Bakemon

7 Which Digimon digivolves to drive the Black Gear out of the flaming Digimon that guards the volcano?

A. Koromon digivolves to Agumon.

B. WereGarurumon digivolves to MetalGarurumon.

C. Biyomon digivolves to Birdramon.

8 When the kids come upon a strange factory that produces electric power, which robotlike Digimon do they free?

A. Numemon

B. Etemon

C. Andromon

9 What does Izzy find inside the strange factory?

A. a chamber with a computer program that runs the entire factory

B. his first Digimon, Motimon

C. a way back to Earth

10 What happens when Izzy accesses the factory's mainframe with his laptop?

A. He mysteriously vanishes.

B. Tentamon digivolves into Kabuterimon.

C. Kuwagamon attacks.

11 Where do the Numemon live?

A. in the sewer

B. in the forest

C. in the ocean

12 What is really weird about Toy Town?

    A. The toys are all broken.

    B. There are no toys in Toy Town.

    C. The toys play with children.

13 Which giant Teddy Bear Digimon captures the kids in Toy Town?

    A. Monzaemon

    B. Numemon

    C. Andromon

14 Which Digimon digivolves into its giant cactus form to defeat the giant Teddy Bear Digimon?

    A. Patamon digivolves to Angemon.

    B. Palmon digivolves to Togemon.

    C. Ikkakumon digivolves to Zudomon.

15 Who decides to climb a mountain by himself to get a better view of the island?

    A. Izzy

    B. Matt

    C. Joe

16 Which Unicorn Type Digimon attacks this Digidestined boy on the mountain?

A. Leomon

B. Unimon

C. Ogremon

17 Sora and Tai show up with which Digimon to help after the Unicorn Type Digimon attacks?

A. Birdramon

B. Bukamon

C. Koromon

18 Who finally digivolves to destroy the Black Gear that has been controlling the Unicorn Type Digimon?

A. Togemon digivolves to Lillymon.

B. Greymon digivolves to MetalGreymon.

C. Gomamon digivolves to Ikkakumon.

THE KID MOST LIKELY TO...

1 The Digidestined child most likely to spring into action is _____.

2 The Digidestined child most likely to try to keep the others safe is _____.

3 The Digidestined child most likely to chose a different path from the others is _____.

4 The Digidestined child most likely to get scared but not tell the others is _____.

5 The Digidestined child most likely to be alone with a computer is _____.

6 The Digidestined child most likely to not quite understand what is going on is _____.

7 The Digidestined child most likely to worry is

_____.

DIGI-GRID
WORD SEARCH

The names of eleven Digimons are hidden in the grid below. Can you find them? Search up, down, backward, forward, and diagonally to find:

Koromon, Biyomon, Yokomon, Patamon, Angemon, Palmon, Greymon, Gomamon, Togemon, Tanemon, Digimon

B	N	Y	T	I	G	I	D	N	Y
I	O	P	A	L	M	O	N	O	N
G	M	A	N	O	N	K	K	M	O
R	I	L	E	O	O	O	Y	A	M
E	G	G	M	R	M	G	O	M	E
Y	I	O	O	O	E	O	K	O	G
M	D	M	N	M	G	I	Y	G	O
O	O	N	T	O	N	G	O	I	T
N	O	M	A	T	A	P	K	O	B

WEAPON MATCH I

Match each Digimon listed on this page with its most powerful weapon

1. MetalGreymon
2. WarGreymon
3. Garurumon
4. WereGarurumon
5. MetalGarurumon
6. Garudamon

A. Wing Blade
B. Wolf Claw
C. Metal Wolf Claw
D. Howling Blaster
E. Giga Blaster
F. Terra Force

1 — _____   2 — _____

3 — _____   4 — _____

5 — _____   6 — _____

WEAPON MATCH II

Match each Digimon shown on this page with its most powerful weapon.

1 — ___

2 — ___

3 — ___

4 — ___

5 — ___

6 — ___

7 — ___

A Nova Blast

B Meteor Wing

C Blue Blaster

D Pepper Breath

E Spiral Twister

F Poison Ivy

G Bubble Blow

DIGI-CROSSWORD

THE CLUES:

Down

1. Mimi wears this type of hat.
2. Tai's sister; she turns out to be the eighth Digidestined child.
4. Greymon's Nova Blast is this type of attack.
5. Gabumon has this on his head.
6. The oldest of the Digidestined children.
7. Where the seven Digidestined children were when they were transported to DigiWorld.
10. The item that transported the seven friends to DigiWorld is known as a _____.
11. In DigiWorld, the children find themselves on the Continent of _____.
13. T.K. is the younger brother of _____.

Across

3. WereGarurumon's weapon.
7. In school, Sora played on this sports team.
8. Kuwagamon looks like a giant red _____.
9. Tai's elementary school.
12. The item that turns good Digimons evil.
14. The first island the seven friends visit in Digi-World.
15. Izzy is a whiz with a _____.

THREE-WAY CREST MATCH

Match each Digidestined child first with
their crest name, then with
the picture of their crest.

1 Tai

____ _

2 Matt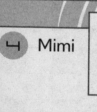

____ _

3 Sora

____ _ ____

4 Mimi

____ _

5 Izzy

____ _

6 T.K.

____ _ __

7 Joe

____ _ ___

H

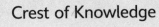
A. Crest of Knowledge

B. Crest of Love

C. Crest of Courage

D. Crest of Reliability

E. Crest of Friendship

F. Crest of Sincerity

G. Crest of Hope

I

J

K

L

M

N

33

DIGI-QUIZ III

Here's your third Digi-Quiz. Some questions are fill-ins, some are true/false, others are multiple choice. Some questions relate to the ones before them, so be sure to read them all in order.

Fill-ins

1 Leomon, a powerful Good Digimon, looks like what kind of animal?

_____

2 What happens to Leomon to turn him evil?

_____

3 Leomon is controlled by the ruler of the bad Digimons. Who is it?

_____

4 Who else joins Leomon in his attack on the Digidestined?

_____

5 What does Devimon do to File Island?

_____

6 Why does Devimon do this to File Island?

_____

7 Where do Tai and Agumon become marooned?

_____

 8 What evil snowman do they encounter there?

_____

 9 How does Izzy communicate with Mimi when she and Palmon are attacked by Suka-mon and Chuumon?

_____

10 What do Sukamon and Chuumon want to do to Mimi?

_____

True/False
Are the following statements true or false?
Circle T for true statements and F for false ones.

 11 Izzy is busy deciphering hieroglyphs in a jungle ruin while Mimi and Tentomon are attacked by Centarumon. T F

 12 Ogremon attacks Joe and Gomamon while they are adrift at sea. T F

 13 Gomamon saves them by digivolving into Garudamon. T F

 14 Sora and Biyomon rescue Joe and his Digimon from their sinking boat. T F

15 Joe and Sora find Bakemon, the ghost Digimon, in a shopping mall. T F

16 T.K. and Patamon find baby Digimons and DigiEggs in Primary Village. T F

17 Elecmon takes care of the Digimons in Primary Village. T F

18 T.K. suggests a game of tag as a way to settle differences between Patamon and Elecmon in Primary Village. T F

19 File Island returns to normal only when the hearts of all Digimons are one. T F

20 The Great Secret of DigiWorld is that every thing in it (even the children) are just bits of data. T F

21 A Digivice can be used to destroy Black Gears. T F

22 The kids hope to return home by defeating Kuwagamon. T F

23 Just before he becomes data and disappears, Devimon reveals that there are other evil Digimons even stronger than he is. T F

24 When Devimon disappears, File Island shatters into many pieces. T F

25 Gennai is the wise old man who offers the seven children advice. T F

Multiple Choice

 26 Where does Gennai tell the kids to go after Devimon disappears?

A. the continent of Server
B. back to Earth
C. the caves on File Island

 27 What will they find there?

A. the eighth Digidestined child
B. a way back home
C. tags and crests hidden there by Devimon

28 What can tags and crests do if they are found?

A. enable the kids' Digimons to digivolve to the next level
B. send the kids back home
C. give the kids incredible powers

 29 Who must the kids defeat to recover the missing tags?

A. Leomon
B. Drimogemon
C. Ogremon

 30 Who do the kids first meet when they arrive on the Continent of Server?

A. Etemon, led by Whamon
B. Pagumon, led by Gazimon
C. Datamon, led by Tyranomon

31 Who are the real inhabitants of Server?

A. the Koromon
B. the Piximon
C. the Vegiemon

32 Who controls the Dark Network?

A. Gekomon
B. Myotismon
C. Etemon

33 What does the leader of the Dark Network use as a weapon?

A. his rock-and-roll guitar
B. his crystal ball
C. his Digivice

34 After escaping from the leader of the Dark Network, what does Tai find in a cave?

A. the Crest of Hope
B. the Crest of Courage
C. the Crest of Love

35 How does Tai know it belongs to him?

A. It has his name on it.
B. It fits into his Digivice.
C. It fits into his tag.

36 What two things do Digimons need to digivolve?

A. Their human partner must be in danger, and they must have lots of energy.

B. They must have five other Digimons plus one human near them.

C. a Digivice and a tag

37 What happens when Tai overfeeds Agumon?

A. He digivolves into the evil MagnaAngemon.

B. He digivolves into the evil SkullGreymon.

C He digivolves into the evil MegaKabuterimon.

38 How do the others stop SkullGreymon?

A. They don't; SkullGreymon just runs out of energy.

B. Gennai helps them.

C. Lillymon stops him.

39 What advice does Gennai give the seven kids when he appears to them in the desert?

A. Leave DigiWorld as quickly as possible.

B. Feed your Digimons as much as you possibly can.

C. Care for your Digimons or they won't digivolve properly.

40 Which famous Digimon trainer teaches the kids' Digimons self-discipline?

A. Piximon

B. Dokugumon

C. Raremon

DIGI-TYPE
FILL-IN

What type of Digimon is each of the Digital Monsters listed below? Choose from the following list: Micro Digimon, Reptile Digimon, Dinosaur Digimon, Android Digimon, Mammal Digimon, Animal Digimon, Bird Digimon, Vegetation Digimon, Insectoid Digimon, Angel Digimon, Sea Mammal Digimon.

1 Koromon_____

2 Agumon_____

3 Greymon_____

4 MetalGreymon_____

5 WarGreymon_____

6 Tsunomon_____

7 Gabumon _____

8 Garurumon_____

9 WereGarurumon_____

10 MetalGarurumon_____

11 Yokomon_____

12 Biyomon_____

WEAPON MATCH III

Match each Digimon listed on this page with its most powerful weapon.

1	Lillymon	A	Marching Fishes
2	MegaKabuterimon	B	Celestial Arrow
3	Gomamon	C	Flower Cannon
4	Gatomon	D	Horn Buster
5	Angewoman	E	Lightning Paw

1 — _____

2 — _____

3 — _____

4 — _____

5 — _____

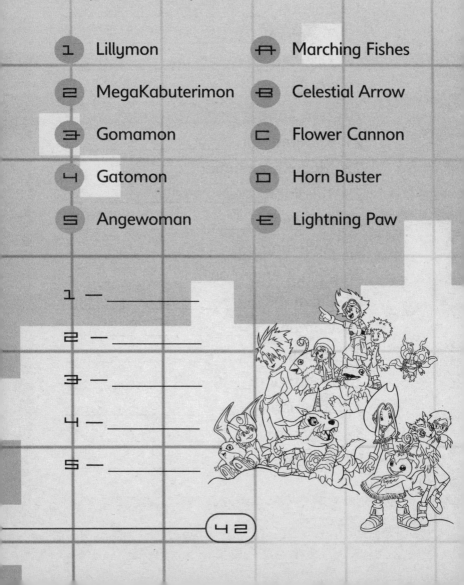

ЩEЯPON MЯTCH IV

Match each Digimon shown on this page with its most powerful weapon.

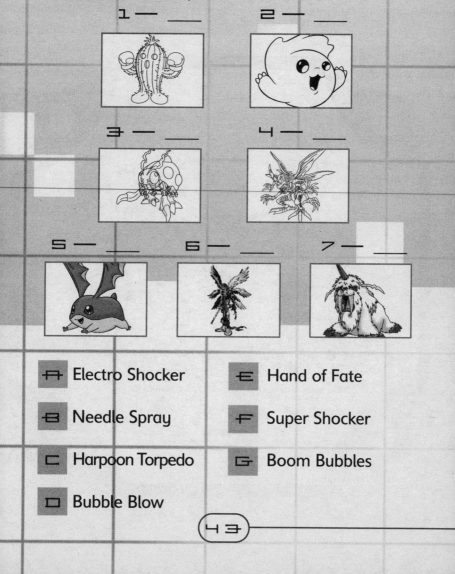

1 — ___

2 — ___

3 — ___

4 — ___

5 — ___

6 — ___

7 — ___

Ꞁ Electro Shocker

ᗺ Needle Spray

Ⲥ Harpoon Torpedo

◻ Bubble Blow

Ⲉ Hand of Fate

Ꞙ Super Shocker

Ꮐ Boom Bubbles

43

WHAT'S THE DIFFERENCE?

Find the ten differences between these two pictures of the seven Digidestined and their Digimons.

IZZY'S SECRET CODE

Izzy uses a secret code to send a serious message through his computer from DigiWorld back to Earth. Use the code key below to find out what this grave warning could be.

Code key
A=Z, B=Y, C=X, D=W, E=V, F=U, G=T, H=S, I=R, J=Q, K=P, L=O, M=N

The Message
GSRH   DLIOW   RH   UFOO   LU   WRTRGZO

_ _ _ _   _ _ _ _ _   _ _   _ _ _ _   _ _

_ _ _ _ _ _ _

NLMHGVIH.   HGZB   ZDZB!!

_ _ _ _ _ _ _ _.   _ _ _ _   _ _ _ _!!

DIGIVOLUTION . . . NOT!

The Digimons below are digivolving. But something is wrong. In each of the groups, one Digimon does not belong in the digivolution. Circle the Digimon who does not belong.

THE DIGIVOLUTIONS CONTINUE...

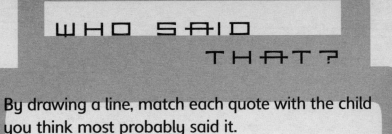

WHO SAID THAT?

By drawing a line, match each quote with the child you think most probably said it.

1 Tai   **A** "People are always saying I'm the coolest."

2 Matt   **B** "I'm into computers and high-end tech stuff."

3 Sora   **C** "I'm probably what you would call the leader."

4 Mimi   **D** "I hope my Digimon doesn't carry any weirdo diseases."

5 Izzy   **E** "This place can be kind of creepy sometimes."

6 T.K.   **F** "My hair gets all frizzy here, and I just hate that, you know?"

7 Joe   **G** "I have to be like the big sister to these guys."

49

DIGI-QUIZ IV

Ready for your next Digi-Quiz? Thought so! This one's a true/false test. Ready? Get set. Go!

1. As Agumon grows, he gains the ability to walk on two legs. T F

2. Datamon is the digivolved form of Togemon. T F

3. Koromon's main weapon is the Terra Force. T F

4. Even though Biyomon is a Bird Type Digimon, she is not very good at flying. T F

5. Tai and Koromon are pulled through a dimensional rift and are transported back to Earth. T F

6. When Tsunomon digivolves into Gabumon, he loses the horn on his head. T F

7. Back on Earth, Tai discovers that Kari is aware of the Digimons. T F

8. Kari is Tai's mother. T F

9. Although Tentomon has insect arms, the hands on his middle set of arms can be used just like human hands. T F

10. When Tai and Agumon return to DigiWorld, they meet up with a new evil Digimon named Devimon. T F

11. When T.K. eats the mushrooms of forgetfulness he can't remember his own name. T F

12. Palmon has a tropical flower on her head. T F

13. Sora is forced to work in the diner run by Vegiemon. T F

14. Vademon tricks Izzy into giving up his tag and crest. T F

15. Mimi is taken to a fortress by the froglike Gekomon who forces her to sing. T F

16. Gennai tells the children that there is an eighth Digidestined child back on Earth. T F

17. Togemon looks like a giant apple tree. T F

18. Kabuterimon is an Insectoid Digimon. T F

19. Digimons can only digivolve if four of them are together in a group. T F

20. The stripe of fur running down Gomamon's back changes color as his mood changes. T F

21. Ikkakumon roars when he is angry. T F

22. WereGarurumon and MetalGarurumon are both Animal Type Digimons. T F

23. Patamon can use his big ears to fly. T F

24. Most of the action in DigiWorld takes place on Folder Island. T F

25. Agumon and Greymon both use the Nova Blast as their main weapons. T F

26. Each tag has a space made to fit a specific crest. T F

27. T.K. is Matt's older brother. T F

28. Kokatorimon turns the boys' Digimons to stone. T F

29. Of the seven friends, Joe knows the most about computers. T F

30. Koromon, Tsunomon, Yokomon, Tanemon, Motimon, Tokomon, and Bukamon all use the Bubble Blow as their main weapon. T F

31 The children need their crests in order for their Digimons to digivolve to the ultimate level. T F

 32 Kari's Digimons are Nyaromon, Salamon, Gatomon, and Angemon. T F

 33 The wise old man who advises the children in DigiWorld is named Gennai. T F

 34 The gateway from DigiWorld back to Earth is in Myotismon's castle. T F

 35 In order to open the gateway between worlds, the children must learn the secret of the ten Digimon cards. T F

 36 Tai finally cracks the secret code that enables the kids to return to Earth. T F

 37 When they journey back to Earth, the kids find themselves transported directly to their homes. T F

 38 The Ultimate form of Motimon is MagnaAngemon. T F

39 Gomamon's main weapon is Marching Fishes. T F

40 Mimi's crest is the Crest of Sincerity. T F

DARK MASTER SCRAMBLE

The Four Dark Masters are trying to take over DigiWorld. To stop them, unscramble each of their names. We've given you the first letter in each case, plus a hint.

1. TELAMADRESMANO M _____

_____

(hint: like iron or steel)

2. HAMOCNINDEARM M _____

_____

(hint: engine, equipment)

3. TEPOPUMPN P _____

_____

(hint: marionette)

4. DEMOPIN P _____

_____

(hint: piper)

THE EIGHTH CHILD

Gennai tells the seven children in Digi-World that there is an eighth Digidestined child back on Earth. To learn her name, answer the following four questions. Then write the FIRST LETTER of each answer in the spaces below.

1   Tai's In-Training Digimon is _____
_____

2   T.K.'s Champion Digimon is _____
_____

3   Joe's crest is the Crest of _____
_____

4   The "wired" member of the group of seven Digidestined children is _____
_____.

The eighth Digidestined child is:

— — — —.

1   2   3   4

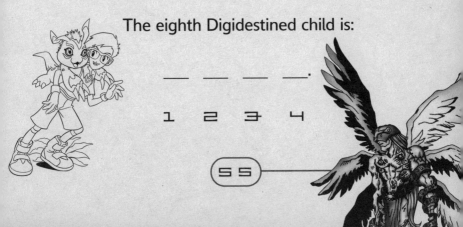

⊓⊓T−T⊓−⊓⊓T,
⊓⊓⊓−T⊓−⊓⊓⊓⊓ II

Connect the dots on this page to meet the most pampered of the Digidestined children. Then connect the dots on each of the next three pages to see this kid's Digimon digivolve.

Connect the dots on this page to meet a Micro Type, In-Training-level Digimon, who is partner to the kid on the previous page.

Connect the dots on this page to meet a Vegetation Type, Rookie-level Digimon, who digivolves
from the Digimon on the previous page.

Connect the dots on this page to meet another Vegetation Type, Champion-level Digimon, who digivolves from the Digimon on the previous page.

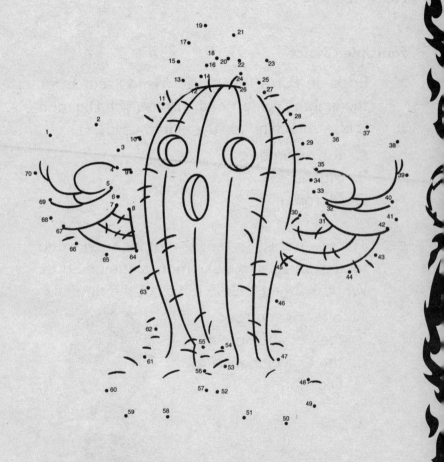

DIGI-QUIZ V

Here's your final Digi-Quiz, and it's a doozy! You've got multiple choice, true/false, fill-ins, and trivia questions. So, hang onto your Digivice . . . Here we go!

Multiple Choice

1 Back on Earth, the seven friends search for the eighth Digidestined child. Which Digimon is also searching for the eighth child?

A. Kuwagamon
B. Myotismon
C. Meramon

2 The seven children realize that four years ago they actually saw a Digimon battle on Earth. What did they believe it was at the time?

A. a terrorist attack
B. the outbreak of war
C. the digivolution of a Digimon

Which Digimon took part in the Digimon battle on Earth four years ago?

A. Motimon
B. Palmon
C. Greymon

 While riding the subway back on Earth, what do the kids pretend their Digimons are?

A. pets
B. backpacks
C. stuffed animals

 When the kids spend all their money on fast food and have no way to continue their journey on Earth, who happens by and picks them up in his van?

A. Sora's cousin Duane
B. Mimi's uncle Morty
C. Matt's brother T.K.

 Who saves Izzy when he accidentally falls off a bridge?

A. Gabumon
B. Tentomon
C. Biyomon

7 Who does Devimon send to Earth to attack the kids?

A. Raremon

B. Gesomon

C. Mammothmon

8 Who knocks Kari's Digivice out the window?

A. her cat

B. Devimon

C. her dog

9 How does Devimon keep track of the eighth Digivice?

A. with a laptop computer

B. with his great mental powers

C. with a stolen tag

10 Who disguises herself as a cat to secretly follow Kari?

A. Gatomon

B. Mimi

C. Agumon

11 Which fire-breathing Digimon comes after Mimi and Sora on Earth?

A. Meramon

B. SkullMeramon

C. Birdramon

12 Which two of Myotismon's henchmen have been partying in the city rather than searching for the eighth Digidestined child?

A. Devimon and Mammothmon

B. Gesomon and Raremon

C. Pumpkinmon and Gotsumon

True or False?

13 When Myotismon finds out that his henchmen have not been searching for the eighth Digidestined child, he blasts them back to DigiWorld. T F

14 Wizardmon finds the eighth Digivice and brings it right to Devimon. T F

15 Gatomon steals Kari's crest. T F

16 Myotismon covers the city in fog, then sends Phantomon and his ghostly minions to search for the eighth child. T F

17 The huge Dinosaur Type Digimon that attacks the kids on Earth is Dark Tyrannomon. T F

18 Gennai tells Izzy that a local radio station is the source of Myotismon's fog barrier. T F

19 Kari admits that she is the eighth Digidestined child and is taken away by Phantomon. T F

20 Gatomon digivolves into Angewomon and hits Myotismon with a Celestial Arrow. T F

21 After Myotismon disappears, the fog barrier goes away. T F

22 Gennai finds a prophecy that says that bats will appear in the sky. T F

Fill-ins

 23 Kari needs her _____ to defeat Myotismon.

 24 Gabumon warp-digivolves into his Ultimate Form of _____.

 25 Myotismon returns as an energy-devouring monster called _____.

 26 The huge land mass in the sky that moves toward the kids is really _____.

 27 When the eight Digidestined kids return to DigiWorld, they find that the ____ _____ are trying to take it over.

 28 The evil team trying to take over DigiWorld consists of MetalSeadramon, Machinedramon, Puppetmon, and _____.

 29 When the kids are attacked by the evil foursome, _____ comes to their rescue.

30 When the kids return to DigiWorld they find themselves on the shores of the ocean domain of _____.

Trivia

 31 How do the kids defeat VenomMyotismon?

_____

 32 How can the kids save Earth?

_____

 33 Who attacks the kids in the ocean domain?

_____

 34 Who do Togemon and Ikkakumon digivolve into to save the kids in the ocean domain?

_____

 35 What caused the problem of evil Digimons in DigiWorld?

_____

 36 What called the eight Digidestined children to DigiWorld to solve the problem?

_____

 37 Once DigiWorld has been set right by the eight children, where do they go?

_____

38 How much time has passed back on Earth during the time they kids were gone in Digi-World?

_____

FASCINATING TRIVIA FACTS

Congratulations! You made it through the whole book and are about to find out what level Digi-fan you have digivolved to: In-Training, Rookie, Champion, or Ultimate. Before you add up your points, here are some more facts any Digi-Expert needs to know.

- ◉ Digimons are artificial life-forms that originated in a computer network.

- ◉ A Digital Monster is created when a self-aware computer virus absorbs various data from a computer network. The virus changes its form, then grows and evolves in the Digi-World.

- ◉ Digimons differ according to the type of information they copied when they were formed. Some Digimons copied shapes of creatures like dinosaurs, insects, unicorns, or dragons.

- ◉ Some Digimons were created from software in karaoke machines, others from dictionary software.

- It is only when Digimons are befriended by humans that they can digivolve into the strongest Digimons.

- Digimons need two things to digivolve: 1) a human partner in danger; and 2) lots of energy.

- The DigiWorld was formed as computer networks spread all over the Earth. As the virtual space that links computers expanded, so did the size of the world in which the Digimons live.

- In the DigiWorld, data takes on substance, sometimes in really strange ways. For example, a telephone booth might suddenly appear in the middle of a secluded beach. Or a waterfall might start pouring down from a clear blue sky!

- The DigiWorld is a shadow of the real world. That means, that whatever happens in the digital world can take some kind of form in the real world!

- The seven Digidestined children who enter DigiWorld are just computer data when they are inside that world.

DIGI-GIGGLES

Did you hear the one about . . . ?

1   How much is five-tomon and five-tomon?

2   Where did the frog Digimon sit?

3   What happened to Mimi's Digimon when she stayed out in the sun too long?

4   Where did Joe read all about the Digimons?

5   What did Matt tell T.K. when he was eating too fast?

6   Which Digimon celebrates Halloween?

ᑎᑎSᗯᗴᖇS

WARNING! If you have turned to this page before doing all the quizzes and puzzles in this book, you're peeking! This probably means you have a Black Gear planted in you someplace that will have to be removed!

Dot-to-Dot, Digi-to-Digi I
p. 1: Tai, p. 2: Koromon, p. 3: Agumon, p. 4: Greymon

Digi-Quiz I
1-A, 2-C, 3-B, 4-B, 5-A, 6-C, 7-A, 8-B, 9-C, 10-C, 11-A, 12-B, 13-A, 14-B, 15-A, 16-C, 17-B, 18-A, 19-B, 20-C

Digi-Match
1-d, 2-a, 3-f, 4-e, 5-b, 6-h, 7-c, 8-g

Digivolution Match-up
1- c,j,r 2- e,h,t 3- a,l,s 4- g,m,p 5- b,i,q 6- d,n,u 7- f,k,o

Digi-Close-up
1) It's the flame coming from Agumon's mouth.
2) It's the horn on Gabumon's head.
3) It's one of Togemon's cactus arms with a boxing glove.
4) It's one of Patamon's wings.
5) It's the markings on Gomamon's eye.
6) It's the bottom of Motimon's ghostly shape.
7) It's one of Garurumon's feathers.
8) It's Biyomon's beak.
9) It's Tsunomon's head fin.
10) It's Birdramon's claw.

Scrambled Names

1) ZUDOMON, 2) LILLYMON, 3) TSUNOMON,
4) IKKAKUMON, 5) AGUMON, 6) GARURUMON,
7) TENTOMON, 8) KABUTERIMON, 9) BUKAMON,
10) MOTIMON

Digi-Grid Picture Search

Digi-Quiz II

1-C, 2-A, 3-B, 4-A, 5-B, 6-A, 7-C, 8-C, 9-A, 10-B, 11-A,
12-C, 13-A, 14-B, 15-C, 16-B, 17-A, 18-C

The Kid Most Likely to . . .

1-Tai, 2-Sora, 3-Matt, 4-T.K., 5-Izzy, 6-Mimi, 7-Joe

Digi-Grid Word Search

Weapon Match I
1-e, 2-f, 3-d, 4-a, 5-b, 6-c

Weapon Match II
1-g, 2-d, 3-a, 4-c, 5-e, 6-b, 7-f

Digi-Crossword
Down: 1-Cowboy, 2-Kari, 4-Fireball, 5-Horn, 6-Joe, 7-Summer camp, 10-Digivice, 11-Server, 13-Matt
Across: 3-Wolf Claw, 7-Soccer, 8-Beetle, 9-Monden, 12-Black Gear, 14-File, 15-Computer

Three-Way Crest Match
1) Tai, c-m
2) Matt, e-h
3) Sora, b-k
4) Mimi, f-i
5) Izzy, a-n
6) T.K., g-l
7) Joe, d-j

Digi-Quiz III
1) a lion
2) He is struck by a Black Gear.
3) Devimon
4) Ogremon
5) He breaks it up into smaller islands.
6) to split up the seven friends so he can defeat each of their Digimons individually
7) in Freeze Land
8) Frigimon
9) through his computer and her Digivice
10) kiss her

11) T	26) A
12) T	27) C
13) F	28) A
14) T	29) B
15) F	30) B
16) T	31) A
17) T	32) C
18) F	33) A
19) T	34) B
20) T	35) C
21) T	36) A
22) F	37) B
23) T	38) A
24) F	39) C
25) T	40) A

Digi-Type Fill-ins

1) Micro Digimon
2) Reptile Digimon
3) Dinosaur Digimon
4) Android Digimon
5) Dinosaur Digimon
6) Micro Digimon
7) Reptile Digimon
8) Mammal Digimon
9) Animal Digimon
10) Android Digimon
11) Micro Digimon
12) Bird Digimon
13) Bird Digimon
14) Bird Digimon
15) Micro Digimon
16) Vegetation Digimon
17) Vegetation Digimon
18) Vegetation Digimon
19) Micro Digimon
20) Insectoid Digimon
21) Insectoid Digimon
22) Insectoid Digimon
23) Micro Digimon
24) Mammal Digimon
25) Angel Digimon
26) Angel Digimon
27) Micro Digimon
28) Sea Mammal Digimon
29) Sea Mammal Digimon
30) Micro Digimon
31) Animal Digimon
32) Animal Digimon
33) Angel Digimon

Weapon Match III
1-c, 2-d, 3-a, 4-e, 5-b,

Weapon Match IV
1-b, 2-d, 3-f, 4-a, 5-g,
6-e, 7-c.

What's the Difference?

Clockwise, from top left:

1. Joe is missing his glasses.
2. Joe is missing his shoulder bag.
3. Sora is missing her bangs.
4. Tai is missing his goggles.
5. Mimi is missing her hat.
6. Tokomon is missing an ear.
7. Tsunomon is missing his horn.
8. Palmon is missing her top curl.
9. Motimon is missing an eye.
10. Bukamon is missing his flame.

Izzy's Secret Code

Izzy's message is:
THIS WORLD IS FULL OF DIGITAL MONSTERS. STAY AWAY!!

Digivolution . . . NOT!

1- Biyomon, 2- Tsunomon, 3- Motimon, 4- Tokomon,
5- Evil Digimon, 6- Gomamon, 7- Kabuterimon

Who Said That?

1-c, 2-a, 3-g, 4-f, 5-b, 6-e, 7-d

Digi-Quiz IV

1-T, 2-F, 3-F, 4-T, 5-T, 6-F, 7-T, 8-F,
9-T, 10-T, 11-F, 12-T, 13-F, 14-T,
15-T, 16-T, 17-F, 18-T, 19-F, 20-T,
21-T, 22-F, 23-T, 24-F, 25-F, 26-T,
27-F, 28-T, 29-F, 30-T, 31-T, 32-F,
33-T, 34-T, 35-T, 36-F, 37-F, 38-F,
39-T, 40-T

Dark Master Scramble
1) MetalSeadramon, 2) Machinedramon,
3) Puppetmon, 4) Piedmon

The Eighth Child
1) Koromon, 2) Angemon, 3) Reliability, 4) Izzy
The eighth Digidestined child is: K A R I

Dot-to-Dot, Digi-to-Digi II
p. 1: T.K., p. 2: Tokomon, p. 3: Patamon, p. 4: Angemon

Digi-Quiz V
1-B, 2-A, 3-C, 4-C, 5-A, 6-B, 7-B, 8-A, 9-C, 10-A, 11-B,
12-C, 13-T, 14-F, 15-F, 16-T, 17-T, 18-F, 19-T, 20-T, 21-F,
22-T, 23-tag and crest, 24-MetalGarurumon, 25-Venom-
Myotismon, 26-DigiWorld, 27-Dark Masters, 28-Piedmon,
29-Piximon, 30-MetalSeadramon, 31- They combine their
attacks as one, and their crests begin to glow. 32- By
returning to DigiWorld and solving the problems there,
33- Shellmon and Scorpiomon, 34- Lillymon and Zudomon,
35- the evil plots of many people, all over the computer
network, forming into one mass of evil, 36- their hope,
37- back to their camp, 38- only three hours

Digi-Giggles
1) Ten-tomon, 2) on the Lilly-mon,
3) She got Tan-emon, 4) in a Buk-amon,
5) "Don't forget to Chuu-mon your food,"
6) Pumpkinmon

WHAT LEVEL DIGI-EXPERT ARE YOU?

So, how did you do? Give yourself one point for each correct answer. Then, using the key below, find out if you are In-Training, a Rookie, a Champion, or an Ultimate Digimon Fan.

0–100 = IN-TRAINING

Keep studying those Digimons. It may take a little time, but soon you will learn enough to digivolve to the next level. Don't worry. You can do it!

101–200 = ROOKIE

Not bad. You've digivolved one level. Keep it up and in no time you'll be Digidestined!

201–300 = CHAMPION

You are a powerful Digimon fan. Your knowledge is vast. Are you sure you didn't grow up in DigiWorld?

OVER 300 = ULTIMATE

You have digivolved to the highest level. You truly are the World's Greatest Digimon Fan!